WHEN
SOMEDAY
COMES

Anne Gigi McCrory

Balboa Press books may be ordered through booksellers or by contacting:

Balboa Press
A Division of Hay House
1663 Liberty Drive
Bloomington, IN 47403
www.balboapress.com
844-682-1282

Because of the dynamic nature of the Internet, any web addresses or links contained in
this book may have changed since publication and may no longer be valid. The views
expressed in this work are solely those of the author and do not necessarily reflect the views
of the publisher, and the publisher hereby disclaims any responsibility for them.

Interior Image Credit: Anne Gigi McCrory

ISBN: 979-8-7652-3174-6 (sc)
ISBN: 979-8-7652-3175-3 (e)

Library of Congress Control Number: 2022913428

Print information available on the last page.

Balboa Press rev. date: 07/29/2022

This book is dedicated to my husband and children, who made difficult choices, demonstrating love and patience during COVID, to keep us all safe;

to all of the families in my classes that worked endlessly to support their children's educational and emotional needs from home, and finally to all the families around the world that had to respond to the many unanswerable questions with love and patience.

You are ALL SUPERHEROES!

When "*someday*" comes, I'll run right out the door.
I'll breathe in the fresh air, without a mask anymore.

"Mom, when can my friends
come inside to play?"
"Someday, my love," she
answers in a soft way.

5

When "Someday" comes,
I'll call my friend Howard.
We'll sit and build Legos
side by side for hours.

"Mom, when can my cousins
and I get together?"
"Someday soon," she whispers
voice as quiet as a feather.

9

When "someday" comes, we'll all have a sleepover. We'll play fun games and invite our grandparents over.

"Mom, when will my indoor sports start again?"
"Someday," she sighs, knowing I miss my friends.

When "someday" comes, I'll shoot hoops with my team. I'll run down the court listening to the fans cheer and scream!

"Mom, when can we go to a restaurant to eat?" "Someday," mom nods, missing *her* special treat.

When "Someday" comes, we'll
sit at a restaurant table.
No cooking or cleaning, just
eating as much as we're able.

"Mom, when can I get close and
give handshakes and hugs?"
Mom looks at me and says, "Come
on over here love bug....."

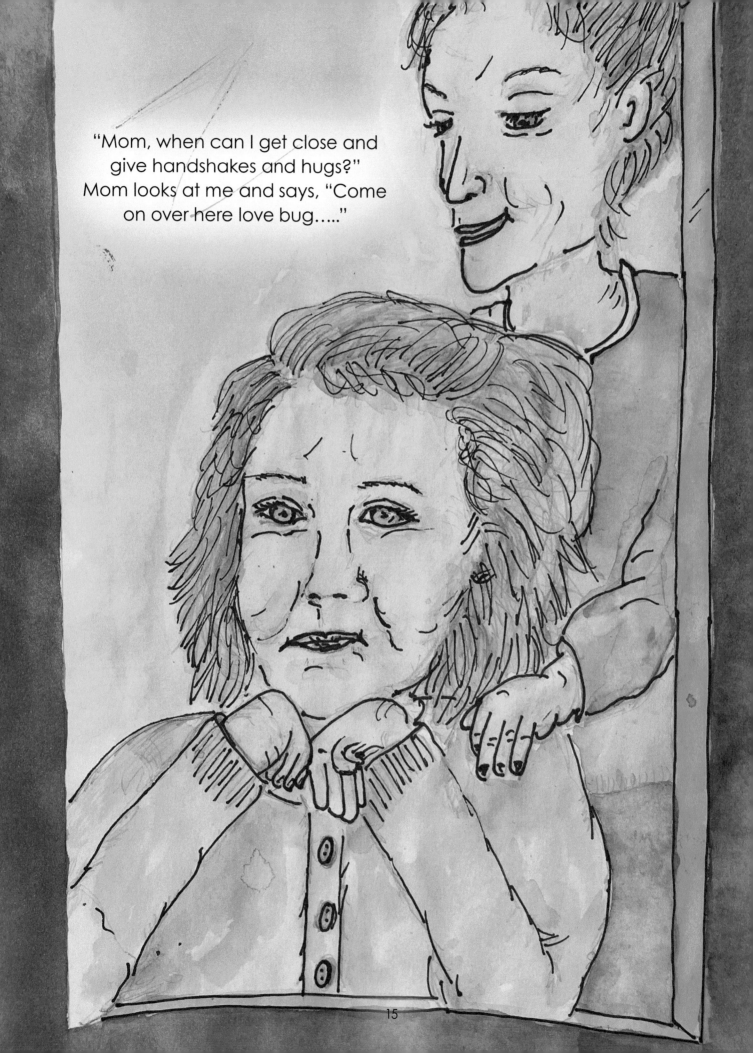

She takes me in her arms and gives me a big squeeze, And says, "Honey, I'd like to talk with you, so listen carefully please." She says, "The somedays you are waiting for are actually quite near. Some may take a little longer to come and some are already here."

"Though they may look
a little different than they
had been in the past,
and we'll have to use our
patience as we sometimes
distance and wear masks,
when somedays come we'll celebrate
them, even if they're small.
We'll remember all the people that
made them possible for us all."

"When someday comes,
we'll remember those who
worked without rest,
to make masks, and vaccines
and bravely provide tests."

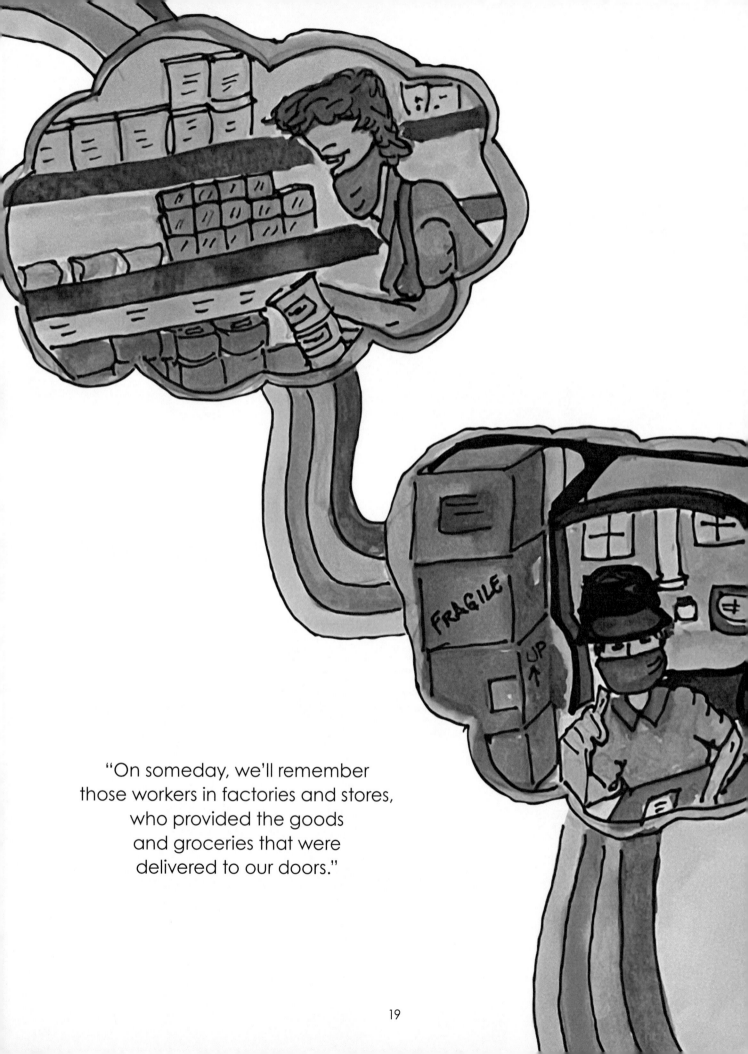

"On someday, we'll remember those workers in factories and stores, who provided the goods and groceries that were delivered to our doors."

We'll think about amazing bus drivers
who got us safely to school and back.
And those caring, devoted teachers
who worked so hard to keep us on track.

"So you see, my love, that SOMEDAY starts right here with me and you. Just remember to be grateful, then we know they will come true."

So I thought about what Mom said, and it all made sense to me.
Somedays WILL come, and we'll give thanks to our community.
With each new day, our somedays will be easier, I see.
I'll wake each day, excited for what changes there will be.

Author Description

Anne McCrory LOVES to wear her many hats as a Teacher, a Mom and a Gigi to her beloved grandbabies. Her degrees in Psychology and Education, her Masters in Literacy, and Reading Specialist Certification were the roots that strengthened her PASSION for reading to children of all ages. Gigi is the name she cherishes and is called by her very loved grandchildren.

Printed in the United States
by Baker & Taylor Publisher Services